The Poetry of Angels

Jeff -
Like angels, we were
sent to watch over
each other.
I am with you,
always.
-Matt
July 16, 1997

THE POETRY

of ANGELS

More than 70 Celestial Poems
to Inspire and Delight

COMPILED BY JEANNE K. HANSON

ILLUSTRATIONS BY PATTI FALZARANO

Crown Trade Paperbacks
New York

Published by Crown Trade Paperbacks, 201 East 50th Street, New York, New York 10022. Member of the Crown Publishing Group.

Random House, Inc. New York, Toronto, London, Sydney, Auckland

CROWN TRADE PAPERBACKS and colophon are trademarks of Crown Publishers, Inc.

Manufactured in the United States of America

Design by Kathy Kikkert

Library of Congress Cataloging-in-Publication Data
The poetry of angels: more than 70 celestial poems to inspire and delight/ compiled by Jeanne K. Hanson; illustrations by Patti Falzarano.—1st pbk. ed.
p.   cm.
1. Angels—Poetry. 2. Angels—Quotations, maxims, etc.
I. Hanson, Jeanne K.
PN6110.A59P64   1995
808.81'9382—dc20   95-34552
                                                     CIP

ISBN 0-517-88623-5

10 9 8 7 6 5 4 3 2 1

First Edition

Introduction

In this book, which I hope you will find beautiful, a different angel graces each of the more than seventy poems. Fierce angels descend here; gentle angels sing through the sky; and quirky angels hover just beyond our view.

These poems span eight centuries, and the angelic vision of each is unique. The earliest angels, envisioned by medieval writers like Guido Guinicelli, may seem at first the most familiar and traditional; their wings are blurred a bit by their distance from us. They break through time and sky as bright light to frighten shepherds in a fifteenth-century lyric, "Now the Most High is born." They shout with glory in "How Grand and how Bright," and they inspire courage in "The Annunciation." In medieval verses, angels are often seen full view, high in the sky, perhaps because the stars were clearer then, and the nights darker.

As we move into the late sixteenth century, with Edmund Spenser's courtly angels and the decorative angels of William Shakespeare, the intensely religious perspective of the medieval period begins to fade. Spenser was by no means irreligious, but his poetry lacks the earlier fear that angels inspired, and, in fact, his angels frequently share stanzas with nymphs. Shakespeare imagined angels in the wings, signaling a farewell to Hamlet, or shining as a metaphor.

Angels are again transformed in the seventeenth-century visions of John Donne, and in the stately roles accorded them by John Milton. Both playful and serious, Donne's angels appear as a "shapeless flame" or serve as messengers blaring trumpets in grandeur. Milton's angels are highly traditional: the armies of heaven formally arrayed, speaking individually into the ear of Adam or Eve.

Later, from the late-eighteenth to mid–nineteenth centuries, poets like William Blake and Emily Dickinson present angels untraditionally, with great individuality. Blake's angels, "glitt'ring in the sky," are quirky, planting flowers or acting almost as companions. Dickinson, too, brings angels close to her, seeing them as heavenly but kindly. They take residence in the house next door; they pick flowers. More traditional are the mostly nineteenth-century poets like Richard Coe, Jr.; their angels dip down to bear souls away and throng 'round the throne of heaven.

Angels in contemporary visions are more anonymous, more radical. Wallace Stevens pictures "the angel of reality" as "half seen," or, in other poems, as divinity within nature. T. S. Eliot's intensely religious *Four Quartets* has forces that feel like angels leaning toward us, attempting to reach us. And Rainer Maria Rilke returns, in his own way, to the terror that some of the medieval angels implied in their time.

And finally, interspersed throughout these changing voices, are the lovely angels of traditional hymns written through the ages. Angels hail in chorus and praise with simple energy. Their music floats through midnights clear, and, on bended wing, they weave a link between heaven and earth, forged in joy.

Choose your own angels, and listen to them.

Angels, in the early morning
May be seen the Dews among,
Stooping - plucking - smiling - flying -
Do the Buds to them belong?

Angels, when the sun is hottest
May be seen the sands among,
Stooping - plucking - sighing - flying -
Parched the flowers they bear along.

—Emily Dickinson

from *Duino Elegies*

Angel! Oh, take it, pluck it, that small-flowered herb of
    healing!
Shape a vase to preserve it. Set it among those joys
not *yet* open to us; in a graceful urn
praise it, with florally-soaring inscriptions . . .

—Rainer Maria Rilke

from *The Faerie Queene*

And is there care in heaven? and is there love
   In heavenly spirits to these creatures base,
That may compassion of their evils move?
   There is: else much more wretched were the case
   Of men, than beasts. But, O! th' exceeding grace
Of highest God, that loves his creatures so,
   And all his works with mercy doth embrace,
That blessed angels he sends to and fro,
To serve to wicked man, to serve his wicked foe.

How oft do they their silver bowers leave,
   To come to succour us, that succour want?
How oft do they with golden pinions cleave
   The flitting skies, like flying pursuivant,
   Against foul fiends to aid us militant?
They for us fight, they watch and duly ward,
   And their bright squadrons round about us plant,
And all for love, and nothing for reward:
O! why should heavenly God to men have such regard?

—Edmund Spenser

from *Holy Sonnets*

At the round earth's imagined corners, blow
Your trumpets, Angels; and arise, arise
From death, you numberless infinities
Of souls, and to your scattered bodies go:
All whom the flood did, and fire shall o'erthrow,
All whom war, dearth, age, agues, tyrannies,
Despair, law, chance hath slain, and you whose eyes
Shall behold God, and never taste death's woe.
But let them sleep, Lord, and me mourn a space;
For, if above all these, my sins abound,
'Tis late to ask abundance of thy grace
When we are there. Here on this lowly ground,
Teach me how to repent; for that's as good
As if thou hadst sealed my pardon with thy blood.

—John Donne

from *Duino Elegies*

Someday, emerging at last from this terrifying vision,
may I burst into jubilant praise to assenting Angels!
May not even one of the clear-struck keys of the heart
fail to respond through alighting on slack or doubtful
or rending strings! May a new-found splendour appear
in my streaming face!

—Rainer Maria Rilke

from *Hamlet*

act 5, scene 2

                    Good-night,
          sweet prince,
And flights of angels sing thee to thy
          rest!

                        —William Shakespeare

A poor - torn heart - a tattered heart -
That sat it down to rest -
Nor noticed that the Ebbing Day
Flowed silver to the West -
Nor noticed Night did soft descend -
Nor Constellation burn -
Intent upon the vision
Of latitudes unknown.

The angels - happening that way
This dusty heart espied -
Tenderly took it up from toil
And carried it to God -
There - sandals for the Barefoot -
There - gathered from the gales -
Do the blue heavens by the hand
Lead the wandering Sails.

—Emily Dickinson

from "Hark! the Herald Angels Sing"

Hark! the herald angels sing,
"Glory to the new-born King!
Peace on earth, and mercy mild,
God and sinners reconciled."
Joyful, all ye nations rise,
Join the triumph of the skies;
With th'angelic host proclaim,
"Christ is born in Bethlehem."
Hark! the herald angels sing,
"Glory to the new-born King!"

—Charles Wesley

from *Anatomy of Melancholy*

Every man hath a good and a bad
angel attending on him in particular,
all his life long.

—Robert Burton

from *Epicedes and Obsequies*

As when an Angel down from heav'n doth fly,
Our quick thought cannot keep him company,
We cannot think, now he is at the Sun,
Now through the Moon, now he through th'air doth run,
Yet when he's come, we know he did repair
To all twixt Heav'n and Earth, Sun, Moon, and Air.
And as this Angel in an instant, knows,
And yet we know, this sudden knowledge grows
By quick amassing several forms of thing,
Which he successively to order brings;
When they, whose slow-pac'd lame thoughts cannot go
So fast as he, think that he doth not so;
Just as a perfect reader doth not dwell,
On every syllable, nor stay to spell,
Yet without doubt, he doth distinctly see
And lay together every A, and B . . .

—John Donne

I never lost as much but twice,
And that was in the sod,
Twice have I stood a beggar
Before the door of God!

Angels - twice descending
Reimbursed my store -
Burglar! Banker - Father!
I am poor once more!

—Emily Dickinson

"Silent Worship"

How sweet to me the silent hour
  When worship to the Lord is given;
For then my soul doth feel the power
  And glory of its God in heaven!
And oh, how sweet the words which come
  From him the Holy Spirit moves;
For 'tis our Father calling home
  His children whom he dearly loves.

And when again a solemn still
  Pervades throughout the meeting-place,
Mine inmost soul is made to thrill
  In the glad song of heavenly grace.
The spirit's song! to Him on high
  Far sweeter than the tuneful voice,
The angels hear the melody,
  And round the throne of love rejoice.

       —Richard Coe, Jr.

from *Duino Elegies*

Who, if I cried, would hear me among the angelic
orders? And even if one of them suddenly
pressed me against his heart, I should fade in the
strength of his stronger existence. For Beauty's nothing
but beginning of Terror we're still just able to bear,
and why we adore it so is because it serenely
disdains to destroy us. Each single angel is terrible.

—Rainer Maria Rilke

from *Hamlet*

act 2, scene 2

What a piece of work is a man, how noble in reason,
how infinite in faculty, in form and moving how express
and admirable, in action how like an angel, in apprehen-
sion how like a god . . .

—William Shakespeare

from "The Hymn"

At last surrounds their sight
A globe of circular light
   That with long beams the shame-fac'd Night array'd;
The helmed Cherubim
And sworded Seraphim
   Are seen in glittering ranks with wings displayed,
Harping in loud and solemn quire
With unexpressive notes to Heav'n's new-born Heir.

Ring out ye crystal spheres,
Once bless our human ears
   (If ye have power to touch our senses so),
And let your silver chime
Move in melodious time;
   And let the bass of Heav'n's deep organ blow;
And with your ninefold harmony
Make up full consort to th'angelic symphony.

—John Milton

Soul, Wilt thou toss again?
By just such a hazard
Hundreds have lost indeed -
But tens have won an all -

Angel's breathless ballot
Lingers to record thee -
Imps in eager Caucus
Raffle for my Soul!

—Emily Dickinson

from *Hymns and Spiritual Songs*

Strange that a harp of thousand strings
Should keep in tune so long!

—Isaac Watts

"Air and Angels"

Twice or thrice had I loved thee,
Before I knew thy face or name;
So in a voice, so in a shapeless flame,
Angels affect us oft, and worshiped be;
    Still when, to where thou wert, I came,
Some lovely glorious nothing I did see.
    But since my soul, whose child love is,
Takes limbs of flesh, and else could nothing do,
    More subtle than the parent is
Love must not be, but take a body too;
    And therefore what thou wert, and who,
        I bid love ask, and now
That it assume thy body I allow,
And fix itself in thy lip, eye, and brow.

Whilst thus to ballast love I thought,
And so more steadily to have gone,
With wares which would sink admiration,
I saw I had love's pinnace overfraught;
　　Every thy hair for love to work upon
Is much too much, some fitter must be sought;
　　For, nor in nothing, nor in things
Extreme and scatt'ring bright, can love inhere.
　　Then as an angel, face and wings
Of air, not pure as it, yet pure doth wear,
　　So thy love may be my love's sphere;
　　　　Just such disparity
As is twixt air and angels' purity,
'Twixt women's love and men's will ever be.

—John Donne

The Angel that presided o'er my birth
Said, "Little creature, form'd of Joy & Mirth,
Go love without the help of any Thing on Earth."

—William Blake

from "It Came Upon a Midnight Clear"

It came upon the midnight clear,
That glorious song of old,
From angels bending near the earth,
To touch their harps of gold:
"Peace on the earth, good will to men
From heav'n's all gracious King,"
The world in solemn stillness lay
To hear the angels sing.

Still thro' the cloven skies they come,
With peaceful wings unfurled;
And still their heav'nly music floats
O'er all the weary world:
Above its sad and lowly plains
They bend on hov'ring wing,
And ever o'er its Babel sounds
The blessed angels sing.

—Edmund H. Sears

from Luke 2: 10–14

And the angel said unto them,
fear not; for behold, I bring you
good tidings of great joy, which
shall be to all people. For unto
you is born this day in the city of
David a Saviour, which is
Christ the Lord. And this
shall be a sign unto you; Ye shall
find the babe wrapped in swaddling
clothes, lying in a manger.
And suddenly there was with
the angel a multitude of heavenly
host praising God, and saying,
glory to God in the highest, and
on earth peace, good will toward men.

from "The Angels,"
Divine Meditations

And since this life our nonage is,
And we in Wardship to thine Angels be,
    Native in heaven's fair Palaces
Where we shall be but denizen'd by thee,
        As th'earth conceiving by the Sun,
            Yields fair diversity,
Yet never knows which course that light doth run,
So let me study, that mine actions be
Worthy their sight, though blind in how they see.

—John Donne

"God's Grandeur"

The world is charged with the grandeur of God.
    It will flame out, like shining from shook foil;
    It gathers to a greatness, like the ooze of oil
Crushed. Why do men then now not reck his rod?
Generations have trod, have trod, have trod;
    And all is seared with trade; bleared,
        smeared with toil;
    And wears man's smudge and shares man's smell:
        the soil
Is bare now, nor can foot feel, being shod.

And for all this, nature is never spent;
    There lives the dearest freshness
        deep down things;
And though the last lights off the black West went
    Oh, morning, at the brown brink eastward,
        springs -
Because the Holy Ghost over the bent
    World broods with warm breast
        and with ah! bright wings.

—Gerard Manley Hopkins

from "For Innocents Day"

The Angel said to Joseph mild
Fly with the Mother and the Child
Out of this Land to Aegipt goe
The heavenly Babe will have it soe.
For that his hower is not yet come,
To dy for mans Redemption.

—Luke Wadding

from *The Merchant of Venice*

act 5, scene 1

How sweet the moonlight sleeps upon this bank!
Here we will sit and let the sounds of music
Creep in our ears: soft stillness and the night
Become the touches of sweet harmony.
Sit, Jessica. Look how the floor of heaven
Is thick inlaid with patines of bright gold:
There's not the smallest orb which thou behold'st
But in his motion like an angel sings,
Still quiring to the young-eyed cherubins.

—William Shakespeare

Except to Heaven, she is naught.
Except for Angels - lone.
Except to some wide-wandering Bee
A flower superfluous blown.

Except for winds - provincial.
Except by Butterflies
Unnoticed as a single dew
That on the Acre lies.

The smallest Housewife in the grass,
Yet take her from the Lawn
And somebody has lost the face
That made Existence - Home!

—Emily Dickinson

"The Annunciation"

Gabriel, fram Hevene King
Sent to the maide swete,
Broughte hire blisful tiding,
And faire he can hire grete:
'Heil! be thu, full of grace aright,
For Godes sone, this Hevene light,
For mannes loven
Wile man becomen,
And taken
Fleas of the maiden bright,
Manken fre for to maken
Of senne and Devles might.'

Mildeliche him gan andsweren
The milde maiden thanne:
'Whiche wise sold ich beren
Child withuten manne?'
Th'angel seide, 'Ne dred thee nought!
Thurw th'Holy Gast shall ben iwrought
This ilche thing,
Wharof tiding
Ich bringe.

All manken wurth ibought
Thurw thy swete childinge,
And ut of pine ibrought.'

Whan the maiden understud,
And th'angels wordes herde,
Mildeliche, with milde mud,
To th'angel hie andswerde:

'Ur Lordes theumaiden, iwis,
Ich am, that her aboven is.
Anenttis me,
Fulfurthed be
Thy sawe,
That ich, sithen his wil is,
Maiden, withuten lawe,
Of moder have the blis.'

.   .   .   .

—Author unknown,
early fourteenth century
(a version of Chaucer's
"Miller's Tale")

Who has not found the Heaven - below -
Will fail of it above -
For Angels rent the House next ours,
Wherever we remove -

—Emily Dickinson

"To Spring"

O thou with dewy locks, who lookest down
Thro' the clear windows of the morning, turn
Thine angel eyes upon our western isle,
Which in full choir hails thy approach, O Spring!

The hills tell each other, and the list'ning
Vallies hear; all our longing eyes are turned
Up to thy bright pavillions: issue forth,
And let thy holy feet visit our clime.

Come o'er the eastern hills, and let our winds
Kiss thy perfumed garments; let us taste
Thy morn and evening breath; scatter thy pearls
Upon our love-sick land that mourns for thee.

O deck her forth with thy fair fingers; pour
Thy soft kisses on her bosom; and put
Thy golden crown upon her languish'd head,
Whose modest tresses were bound up for thee!

—William Blake

from *Paradise Lost*

The Angel ended, and in Adam's ear
So charming left his voice that he awhile
Thought him still speaking, still stood
   fix'd to hear.

—John Milton

from "Angels From the Realms of Glory"

Angels, from the realms of glory,
Wing your flight o'er all the earth;
Ye who sang creation's story,
Now proclaim Messiah's birth:
Come and worship, Come and worship,
Worship Christ, the newborn King.

—James Montgomery

from *Four Quartets*

Time and the bell have buried the day,
The black cloud carries the sun away.
Will the sunflower turn to us, will the clematis
Stray down, bend to us; tendril and spray
Clutch and cling?
Chill
Fingers of yew be curled
Down on us? After the kingfisher's wing
Has answered light to light, and is silent, the light is still
At the still point of the turning world.

—T. S. Eliot

Wait till the Majesty of Death
Invests so mean a brow!
Almost a powdered Footman
Might dare to touch it now!

Wait till in Everlasting Robes
That Democrat is dressed,
Then prate about "Preferment" -
And "Station," and the rest!

Around this quiet Courtier
Obsequious Angels wait!
Full royal is his Retinue!
Full purple is his state!

A Lord, might dare to lift the Hat
To such a Modest Clay
Since that My Lord, "the Lord of Lords"
Receives unblushingly!

—Emily Dickinson

"Angel Surrounded by Paysans"

One of the countrymen:

>   There is
>   A welcome at the door to which no one comes?

The Angel:

>   I am the angel of reality,
>   Seen for a moment standing in the door.
>
>   I have neither ashen wing nor wear of ore
>   And live without a tepid aureole,
>
>   Or stars that follow me, not to attend,
>   But, of my being and its knowing, part,
>
>   I am one of you and being one of you
>   Is being and knowing what I am and know.
>
>   Yet I am the necessary angel of earth,
>   Since, in my sight, you see the earth again,

Cleared of its stiff and stubborn, man-locked set,
And, in my hearing, you hear its tragic drone

Rise liquidly in liquid lingerings,
Like watery words awash; like meanings said

By repetitions of half-meaning. Am I not,
Myself, only half a figure of a sort,

A figure half seen, or seen for a moment, a man
Of the mind, an apparition apparelled in

Apparels of such lightest look that a turn
Of my shoulder and quickly, too quickly, I am gone?

—Wallace Stevens

from "Sonnets from the Portuguese"

When our two souls stand up erect and strong,
Face to face, silent, drawing nigh and nigher,
Until the lengthening wings break into fire
At either curved point—what bitter wrong
Can the earth do to us, that we should not long
Be here contented? Think. In mounting higher,
The angels would press on us and aspire
To drop some golden orb of perfect song
Into our deep, dear silence. Let us stay
Rather on earth, Beloved—where the unfit
Contrarious moods of men recoil away
And isolate pure spirits, and permit
A place to stand and love in for a day,
With darkness and the death-hour rounding it.

—Elizabeth Barrett Browning

Why - do they shut Me out of Heaven?
Did I sing - too loud?
But - I can say a little "Minor"
Timid as a Bird!

Wouldn't the Angels try me -
Just - once - more -
Just - see - if I troubled them -
But don't - shut the door!

Oh, if I - were the Gentleman
In the "White Robe" -
And they - were the little Hand - that knocked -
Could - I - forbid?

—Emily Dickinson

"The Unknown God"

Far up the dim twilight fluttered
      Moth-wings of vapor and flame:
The lights danced over the mountains,
      Star after star they came.

The lights grew thicker unheeded,
      For silent and still were we;
Our hearts were drunk with a beauty
      Our eyes could never see.

              —AE
              (George William Russell)

"Verses"

"Spirit, leave thine house of clay;
        Lingering Dust, resign thy breath!
Spirit, cast thy chains away;
        Dust, be thou dissolved in death!"

Thus thy Guardian Angel spoke,
        As he watched thy dying bed;
As the bonds of life he broke,
        And the ransomed captive fled.

"Prisoner, long detained below;
        Prisoner, now with freedom blest;
Welcome, from a world of woe,
        Welcome to a land of rest!"

Thus thy Guardian Angel sang,
        As he bore thy soul on high,
While with hallelujahs rang
        All the region of the sky . . .

—James Montgomery

from "Prothalamion"

Eftsoons the nymphs, which now had flowers their fill,
Ran all in haste to see that silver brood
As they came floating on the crystal flood;
Whom when they saw, they stood amazed still
Their wondering eyes to fill;
Them seemed they never saw a sight so fair,
Of fowls so lovely that they sure did deem
Them heavenly born, or to be that same pair
Which through the sky draw Venus' silver team;
For sure they did not seem
To be begot of any earthly seed,
But rather angels, or of angels' breed;
Yet were they bred of summer's-heat, they say,
In sweetest season, when each flower and weed
The earth did fresh array;
So fresh they seemed as day,
Even as their bridal day, which was not long:
      Sweet Thames run softly, till I end my song.

—Edmund Spenser

God permits industrious Angels -
Afternoons - to play -
I met one - forgot my Schoolmates -
All - for Him - straightway -

God calls home - the Angels - promptly -
At the Setting Sun -
I missed mine - how *dreary* - *Marbles* -
After playing *Crown!*

—Emily Dickinson

from "While Shepherds Watched"

While shepherds watched their flocks by night,
All seated on the ground,
The angel of the Lord came down,
And glory shone around.

"Fear not," said he for mighty dread
Had seized their troubled minds
"Glad tidings of great joy I bring,
To you and all mankind.

"To you in David's town this day,
Is born of David's line
The Savior, who is Christ the Lord,
And this shall be the sign.

"The heav'nly Babe you there shall find,
To human view displayed,
All meanly wrapp'd in swathing bands
And in a manger laid."

Thus spake the seraph and forthwith
Appear'd a shining throng
Of angels, praising God, who thus
Address'd their joyful song:

"All glory be to God on high,
And to the earth be peace;
Good will henceforth from heav'n to men
Begin and never cease."

—Nahum Tate

from "Woman Looking at a Vase of Flowers"

It was as if thunder took form upon
The piano, that time: the time when the crude
And jealous grandeurs of sun and sky
Scattered themselves in the garden, like
The wind dissolving into birds,
The clouds becoming braided girls.
It was like the sea poured out again
In east wind beating the shutters at night.

—Wallace Stevens

from "Carol of the Birds"

Angels and shepherds, birds of the sky,
Come where the Son of God doth lie;
Christ on earth with man doth dwell,
Join in the shout, "Noel, Noel!"

—Traditional

from *Paradise Lost*

So spake our mother Eve, and Adam heard,
Well pleased, but answered not; for now too nigh
The archangel stood, and from the other hill
To their fixed station, all in bright array,
The cherubim descended; on the ground,
Gliding meteorous, as evening mist,
Risen from a river, o'er the marish glides,
And gathers ground fast at the labourer's heel,
Homeward returning. High in front advanced,
The brandished sword of God before them blazed,
Fierce as a comet which with torrid heat
And vapour as the Libyan air adust
Began to parch that temperate clime; whereat

In either hand the hastening angel caught
Our lingering parents, and to the eastern gate
Led them direct, and down the cliff as fast
To the subjected plain; then disappeared.
They, looking back, all the eastern side beheld
Of Paradise, so late their happy seat,
Waved over by that flaming brand; the gate
With dreadful faces thronged, and fiery arms:
Some natural tears they dropped, but wiped them soon;
The world was all before them, where to choose
Their place of rest, and Providence their guide;
They, hand in hand, with wandering steps and slow
Through Eden took their solitary way.

—John Milton

from *Duino Elegies*

Every Angel is terrible. Still, though, alas!
I invoke you, almost deadly birds of the soul,
knowing what you are.

—Rainer Maria Rilke

Good Night! Which put the Candle out?
A jealous Zephyr - not a doubt -
Ah, friend, you little knew
How long at that celestial wick
The Angels - labored diligent -
Extinguished - now - for you!

It might - have been the Light House spark -
Some Sailor - rowing in the Dark -
Had importuned to see!
It might - have been the waning lamp
That lit the Drummer from the Camp
To purer Reveille!

—Emily Dickinson

"Israfel"

In Heaven a spirit doth dwell
      "Whose heart-strings are a lute;"
None sing so wildly well
As the angel Israfel,
And the giddy stars (so legends tell)
Ceasing their hymns, attend the spell
      Of his voice, all mute.

Tottering above
      In her highest noon,
      The enamoured moon
Blushes with love,
      While, to listen, the red levin
      (With the rapid Pleiads, even,
      Which were seven,)
      Pauses in Heaven.

And they say (the starry choir
     And the other listening things)
That Israfelis fire
Is owing to that lyre
     By which he sits and sings—
The trembling living wire
     Of those unusual strings.

But the skies that angel trod,
     Where deep thoughts are a duty—
Where Love's a grown-up God—
     Where the Houri glances are
     Imbued with all the beauty
     Which we worship in a star.

—Edgar Allan Poe

from *Of Goodness*

The desire of power in excess caused the angels to fall;
the desire of knowledge in excess caused man to fall.

—Francis Bacon

"Once in a Saintly Passion"

Once in a saintly passion
   I cried with desperate grief,
"O Lord, my heart is black with guile,
   Of sinners I am chief."
Then stooped my guardian angel
   And whispered from behind,
"Vanity, my little man,
   You're nothing of the kind."

                        —James Thomson

With happiness stretch'd across the hills
In a cloud that dewy sweetness distills,
With a blue sky spread over with wings
And a mild sun that mounts & sings,
With trees & fields full of Fairy elves
And little devils who fight for themselves—
Rememb'ring the Verses that Hayley sung
When my heart knock'd against the root of my tongue—
With Angels planted in Hawthorn bowers
And God himself in the passing hours,
With Silver Angels across my way
And Golden Demons that none can stay,
With my Father hovering upon the wind.

—William Blake

To fight aloud, is very brave -
But *gallanter*, I know
Who charge within the bosom
The Cavalry of Woe -

Who win, and nations do not see -
Who fall - and none observe -
Whose dying eyes, no Country
Regards with patriot love -

We trust, in plumed procession
For such, the Angels go -
Rank after Rank, with even feet -
And Uniforms of Snow.

—Emily Dickinson

from "How Grand and how Bright"

How grand and how bright that wonderful night
      When angels to Bethlehem came,
They burst forth like fires and they shot their loud lyres
      And mingled their sound with the flame.

The Shepherds were amazed, the pretty lambs gazed
      At darkness thus turned into light,
No voice was there heard, from man, beast nor bird,
      So sudden and solemn the sight.

And then when the sound re-echoed around,
      The hills and the dales awoke,
The moon and the stars stopt their fiery cars
      And listened while Gabriel spoke.

I bring you, said he, from that glorious tree
      A message both gladsome and good,
Our Saviour is come to the world as his home,
      But he lies in a manger of wood.

At mention of this, the source of all bliss,
      The angels sang loudly and long,
They soared to the sky beyond mortal eye,
      But left us the words of their song.

—Author unknown

from "The Kingdom of God"

The angels keep their ancient places;
Turn but a stone, and start a wing!
'Tis ye, 'tis your estranged faces,
That miss the many-splendoured thing.

—Francis Thompson

"The Angel"

I dreamt a Dream! what can it mean?
And that I was a maiden Queen,
Guarded by an Angel mild:
Witless woe was ne'er beguil'd!

And I wept both night and day,
And he wip'd my tears away,
And I wept both day and night,
And hid from him my heart's delight.

So he took his wings and fled;
Then the morn blush'd rosy red;
I dried my tears, & arm'd my fears
With ten thousand shields and spears.

Soon my Angel came again:
I was arm'd, he came in vain;
For the time of youth was fled,
And grey hairs were on my head.

—William Blake

from "Angels We Have Heard on High"

Angels we have heard on high,
Sweetly singing o'er the plains;
And the mountains in reply
Echoing their joyous strains.

. . . .

Come to Bethlehem, and see
Him whose birth the angels sing;
Come adore on bended knee,
Christ, the Lord, our newborn King.

. . . .

—Traditional

from "Sunday Morning"

What is divinity if it can come
Only in silent shadows and in dreams?
Shall she not find in comforts of the sun,
In pungent fruit and bright, green wings, or else
In any balm or beauty of the earth,
Things to be cherished like the thought of heaven?
Divinity must live within herself:
Passions of rain, or moods in falling snow;
Grievings in loneliness, or unsubdued
Elations when the forest blooms; gusty
Emotions on wet roads on autumn nights;
All pleasures and all pains, remembering
The bough of summer and the winter branch.
These are the measures destined for her soul.

—Wallace Stevens

"Song"

Fresh from the dewy hill, the merry year
Smiles on my head, and mounts his flaming car;
Round by young brows the laurel wreathes a shade,
And rising glories beam around my head.

My feet are wing'd, while o'er the dewy lawn
I meet my maiden, risen like the morn:
Oh bless those holy feet, like angels' feet;
Oh bless those limbs, beaming with heav'nly light!

Like as an angel glitt'ring in the sky
In times of innocence and holy joy;
The joyful shepherd stops his grateful song
To hear the music of an angel's tongue.

So when she speaks, the voice of Heaven I hear:
So when we walk, nothing impure comes near;
Each field seems Eden, and each calm retreat;
Each village seems the haunt of holy feet.

But that sweet village, where my black-ey'd maid
Closes her eyes in sleep beneath night's shade,
Whene'er I enter, more than mortal fire
Burns in my soul, and does my song inspire.

—William Blake

A Wife - at Daybreak I shall be -
Sunrise - Hast thou a Flag for me?
At Midnight, I am but a Maid,
How short it takes to make a Bride -
Then - Midnight, I have passed from thee
Unto the East, and Victory -

Midnight - Good Night! I hear them call,
The Angels bustle in the Hall -
Softly my Future climbs the Stair,
I fumble at my Childhood's prayer
So soon to be a Child no more -
Eternity, I'm coming - Sir,
Savior - I've seen the face - before!

—Emily Dickinson

"The White Paternoster"

Matthew, Mark, Luke, and John,
Bless the bed that I lie on.
Four corners to my bed,
Four angels at my head,
One to watch, and one to pray,
And two to bear my soul away.

—Author unknown

from *Duino Elegies*

Angel: suppose there's a place we know nothing about,
   and there,
on some indescribable carpet, lovers showed all that here
they're for ever unable to manage—their daring
lofty figures of heart-flight,
their towers of pleasure, their ladders,
long since, where ground never was, just quiveringly
propped by each other,—suppose they could
   manage it there,
before the spectators ringed round,
   the countless unmurmuring dead:
would not the dead then fling their last,
   their for ever reserved,
ever-concealed, unknown to us, ever-valid
coins of happiness down before the at last
truthfully smiling pair on the quietened
carpet?

—Rainer Maria Rilke

"To the Evening Star"

Thou fair-hair'd angel of the evening,
Now, whilst the sun rests on the mountains, light
Thy bright torch of love; thy radiant crown
Put on, and smile upon our evening bed!
Smile on our loves, and, while thou drawest the
Blue curtains of the sky, scatter thy silver dew
On every flower that shuts its sweet eyes
In timely sleep. Let thy west wind sleep on
The lake; speak silence with thy glimmering eyes,
And wash the dusk with silver. Soon, full soon,
Dost thou withdraw; then the wolf rages wide,
And the lion glares thro' the dun forest:
The fleeces of our flocks are cover'd with
Thy sacred dew: protect them with thine influence.

—William Blake

"Of the Gentle Heart"

Within the gentle heart Love shelters him,
      As birds within the green shade of the grove.
Before the gentle heart, in Nature's scheme,
      Love was not, nor the gentle heart ere Love.
         For with the sun, at once,
      So sprang the light immediately; nor was
         Its birth before the sun's.
And Love hath his effect in gentleness
      Of very self; even as
Within the middle fire the heat's excess.

The fire of Love comes to the gentle heart
      Like as its virtue to a precious stone;
To which no star its influence can impart
      Till it is made a pure thing by the sun:
         For when the sun hath smit
From out its essence that which there was vile,
         The star endoweth it.
And so the heart created by God's breath
      Pure, true, and clean from guile,
A woman, like a star, enamoureth.

.   .   .   .

God, in the understanding of high Heaven,
        Burns more than in our sight the living sun,
There to behold His face unveil'd is given;
        And Heaven, whose will is homage paid to One,
            Fulfils the things which live
In God, from the beginning excellent.
                So should my lady give
That truth which in her eyes is glorified,
            On which her heart is bent,
To me whose service waiteth at her side.

My lady, God shall ask, "What dared'st thou?"
        (When my soul stands with all her acts review'd;)
"Thou passed'st Heaven, into My sight, as now,
        To make Me of vain love similitude.
            To Me doth praise belong.
And to the Queen of all the realm of grace
        Who endeth fraud and wrong."
Then may I plead: "As though from Thee he came,
        Love wore an angel's face:
Lord, if I loved her, count it not my shame."

                            —Guido Guinicelli

Adrift! A little boat adrift!
And night is coming down!
Will *no* one guide a little boat
Unto the nearest town?

So Sailors say - on yesterday -
Just as the dusk was brown
One little boat gave up its strife
And gurgled down and down.

So Angels say - on yesterday -
Just as the dawn was red
One little boat - o'erspent with gales -
Retrimmed its masts - redecked its sails -
And shot - exultant on!

—Emily Dickinson

from *Duino Elegies*

Angels, (they say) are often unable to tell
whether they move among living or dead. The eternal
torrent whirls all the ages through either realm
for ever, and sounds above their voices in both.

—Rainer Maria Rilke

from "Now the Most High is born"

Angelus inquit pastoribus,
'Nunc natus est Altissimus.'

Upon a night an aungell bright
Pastoribus apparuit,
And anone right, thurgh Goddes might,
Lux magna illis claruit:
For love of us
(Scripture seith thus)
Nunc natus est Altissimus.

And of that light that was so bright
Hii valde timuerunt;
A signe of blis to us it is,
Hec lux quam hii viderunt:
For love of us
(Scripture seith thus)
Nunc natus est Altissimus.

'Drede ye nothing, grete joy I bringe,
Quod erit omni populo,
Forwhy to you Christe is borne nowe,
Testante evangelio.'
For love of us
(Scripture seith thus)
Nunc natus est Altissimus.

.   .   .   .

Nowe lete us singe with angelis,
'Gloria, in altissimis!'
That we may come unto that blis
Ubi partus est virginis,
For love of us
(Scripture seith thus)
Nunc natus est Altissimus.

—James Ryman

Forever honored by the Tree
Whose Apple Winterworn
Enticed to Breakfast from the Sky
Two Gabriels Yestermorn.

They registered in Nature's Book
As Robins - Sire and Son -
But Angels have that modest way
To screen them from Renown.

—Emily Dickinson

from *Elegies*

Women are all like Angels; the fair be
Like those which fell to worse; but such as thee,
Like to good Angels, nothing can impair:
'Tis less grief to be foul, than to have been fair.
For one nights revels, silk and gold we choose,
But, in long journeys, cloth, and leather use.
Beauty is barren oft; best husbands say. . . .

—John Donne

"To All Angels and Saints"

Oh glorious spirits, who after all your bands
See the smooth face of God without a frown
     Or strict commands;
Where ev'ry one is king, and hath his crown,
If not upon his head, yet in his hands:

Not out of envie or maliciousnesse
Do I forbear to crave your speciall aid:
     I would addresse
My vows to thee most gladly, Blessed Maid,
And Mother of my God, in my distresse.

Thou art the holy mine, whence came the gold,
The great restorative for all decay
     In young and old;
Thou art the cabinet where the jewell lay:
Chiefly to thee would I my soul unfold:

But now, alas, I dare not; for *our* King,
Whom we do all joyntly adore and praise,
                Bids no such thing:
And where his pleasure no injunction layes,
('Tis your own case) ye never move a wing.

All workship is prerogative, and a flower
Of his rich crown, from whom lyes no appeal
                At the last houre;
Therefore we dare not from his garland steal,
To make a posie for inferiour power.

Although then others court you, if ye know
What's done on earth, we shall not fare the worse
                Who do not so;
Since we are ever ready to disburse,
If any one our Masters hand can show.

                    —George Herbert

The Gentian weaves her fringes -
The Maple's loom is red -
My departing blossoms
        Obviate parade.

A brief, but patient illness -
An hour to prepare,
And one below this morning
Is where the angels are -
It was a short procession,
The bobolink was there -
An aged Bee addressed us -
And then we knelt in prayer -
We trust that she was willing -
We ask that we may be.
Summer - Sister - Seraph!
Let us go with thee!

In the name of the Bee -
And of the Butterfly -
And of the Breeze - Amen!

—Emily Dickinson

"A Woman's Shortcomings"

Unless you can love, as the angels
   may,
With the breadth of heaven betwixt
   you;
Unless you can dream that his faith is
   fast,
Through behoving and unbehoving;
Unless you can die when the dream is past—
Oh, never call it loving!

—Robert Browning

"Wonder"

How like an angel came I down!
How bright are all things here!
When first among his works I did appear,
O how their glory me did crown!
The world resembled his eternity,
In which my soul did walk,
And everything that I did see
Did with me talk.

The skies in their magnificence,
The lively, lovely air;
O how divine, how soft, how sweet, how fair!
The stars did entertain my sense,
And all the works of God so bright and pure,
So rich and great did seem,
As if they ever must endure,
In my esteem.

A native health and innocence
              Within my bones did grow,
And while my God did all his glories show,
              I felt a vigor in my sense
That was all Spirit. I within did flow
              With seas of life like wine;
I nothing in the world did know
              But 'twas divine.

Harsh ragged objects were concealed,
              Oppression's tears and cries,
Sins, griefs, complaints, dissensions, weeping eyes,
              Were hid; and only things revealed
Which heavenly spirits and the angels prize.
              The state of innocence
And bliss, not trades and poverties,
              Did fill my sense.

The streets were paved with golden stones,
        The boys and girls were mine,
O how did all their lovely faces shine!
        The sons of men were holy ones.
Joy, beauty, welfare did appear to me
            And everything which here I found
While like an angel I did see,
            Adorned the ground.

—Thomas Traherne

from "Mans medley"

Heark, how the birds do sing,
　　　　　And woods do ring.
All creatures have their joy: and man hath his.
　　　Yet if we rightly measure,
　　　　　Mans joy and pleasure
Rather thereafter, then in present, is.

　　　To this life things of sense
　　　　　Make their pretence:
In th' other, Angels have a right by birth:
　　　Man ties them both alone,
　　　　　And makes them one,
With th' one hand touching heav'n, with th' other, earth.

　　　　　　　—George Herbert

Permissions

Jeanne K. Hanson received a master's degree in English Literature from Harvard University. A literary agent for more than ten years, she lives in Minneapolis with her husband and two college-age children—when they are home.

Patti Falzarano's work has appeared in magazines such as *Glamour* and *House and Garden,* and in books, including *Celebrating Family Traditions* and *Gingerbread Houses.* She lives in New Jersey with her husband and two sons.